Agile
Process
Innovation

HACKING LEAN SIX SIGMA
TO MAXIMIZE RESULTS

By: Jay Arthur

Printed in the United States of America

First Printing, 2019

Library of Congress Control Number: 2014916863
Lifestar Publishing
2696 S Colorado Blvd, Ste 555
Denver, CO 80222

TABLE OF CONTENTS

TRENDS AFFECTING LEAN SIX SIGMA

1. Changes in the U.S. economy

Motorola developed Six Sigma for a manufacturing, but this is no longer a main part of the economy. Service industries such as healthcare do not need all the tools in the Six Sigma toolkit. Trying to teach services everything needed for jobs in manufacturing is foolish and unnecessary. It's *overproduction.*

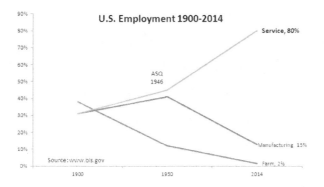

2. Continuous, Accelerating, Disruptive Change

Growing up in the 1950s, everything seemed stable. Then in the 1960s we had civil rights, women's rights, the Vietnam war, Haight-Ashbury, the space race and the internet. I went to work for

1

Mountain Bell, one of the Baby Bells, in 1973. It was a cash cow that had been solid and unchanging for over 50 years. I worked at Bell Labs from 1975-1978 using Unix which became the operating system for internet servers all over the world. Apple launched their first computer in the late 70s; IBM followed in the early 80s. Moore's law has been doubling the speed and halving the cost of computing for over 30 years with no end in sight. Bandwidth has been doubling in speed and having in cost ever nine months. My smart phone has more computing power and storage than the entire planet when I started working.

Cable companies started wiring homes for high-speed data. Cell phones began to replace landline phones. While the Justice Department was dismantling AT&T, technological disruption was jackhammering its very foundation. The phone company couldn't see or embrace the changes. GE, once the shining star of Six Sigma, has fallen in to trouble. Motorola, the birthplace of Six Sigma, fell from grace in the cell phone market to be replaced by iPhones and Galaxies. Google launched in 1998.

3. Agile Methodologies

Faced with continuous, accelerating, disruptive change, businesses have had to find ways to respond. Surprisingly, they found a faster, better, cheaper path in Information Technologies (IT) of all places.

While Moore's law was making hardware massively more powerful and productive, software productivity had barely improved since the 1960s. In 2001, a group of software engineers banded together to adapt Lean principles to software engineering. They called this new methodology *Agile*.

In the last decade, *Agile* methodologies have worked their way into HR, procurement, sales, marketing and other business functions. In the last few years, the Harvard Business Review has published many articles about the power of *Agile*.

Lean Six Sigma is anything but agile. Spending months training Black Belts to train Green Belts and waiting months or years for results is no longer acceptable. This might have been possible in the last century, but it won't work for 21st Century quality. We need to adapt Agile to Lean Six Sigma.

BETTER, FASTER AND CHEAPER

In 1990, when I first got involved in quality improvement at US West, one of the Baby Bells, I told my boss that quality was about getting *better, faster and cheaper*. In typical Bell System fashion, he told me that I could have *any two of the three*: better and faster, but not cheaper; faster and cheaper, but not better; or better and cheaper, but not faster.

> *The basic goal is to do things faster, cheaper, safer, better.*
>
> — Mark Albrecht, director of the White House
> National Space Council, 1990

I was in one of the first groups trained in Total Quality Management (TQM) that would later evolve into Six Sigma. I was trained as a trainer and we started training lots of team leaders. We started hundreds of teams. *A year later, only three teams had delivered any results.* The rest were stuck or had been abandoned. I see this often in companies that launch Six Sigma.

Even though our training was excellent, it didn't seem to translate into fixing the phone company. I decided to use the principles of TQM on itself and treat each failed team as a *defect*. Then I started to apply the tools of quality to team failures. I did some root cause analysis. Here's what I found:

- The five-day training and big 3-ring binders telegraphed the message that this was difficult and time consuming (not true).

  Solution: I created a 24-page "Coloring book" to simplify learning the key tools and I used Accelerated Learning methods to teach them in four hours while simultaneously solving a business problem or two. Download the current version from www.qimacros.com/pdf/six-sigma-action-plan.pdf.

- Teams were *formed* before they knew what problem they needed to solve which caused teams to flounder. They usually wanted to fix someone else's process—their suppliers, customers or management, not their own processes.

IT"S THEIR FAULT

SUPPLIERS   CUSTOMERS

Solution: I started using data analysis to *laser focus the improvement before we picked the team.* I found that if I could create a control chart and Pareto charts of defects, mistakes or errors, I could ensure the team's success. And I could often do this in a few hours or days, not weeks or months. QI Macros Data Mining Wizard will now do this in *seconds.* Automation is one of the keys to *Agile.*

- Teams met for only one hour a week, which slowed progress to a halt and violated two Lean principles: *eliminate delays and institute one-piece flow.*

  Solution: I switched to two-hour root cause sessions based on the data analysis.

- I developed some rules such as:

  o Whalebone diagramming (instead of fishbone) is a sure sign of failure to properly focus the improvement.

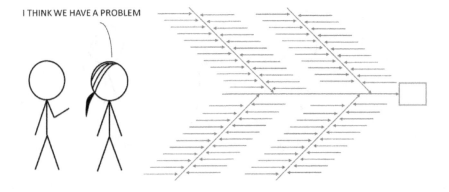

I THINK WE HAVE A PROBLEM

o Never start a team that can't succeed.

o Let data analysis pick the problem to be solved (never brainstorm).

And others that you'll discover in this book.

FOOL-PROOF SIX SIGMA RECIPE

It was midway through my second year as a team leader that I stumbled upon a fool-proof recipe for Six Sigma success. The head of our division thought there were too many false fire alarms in our building. I sat down with the building manager and we reviewed the data and created our first successful improvement story *in an afternoon*.

That's when I learned it was possible to use the tools to solve problems in hours, not weeks, months or years. I began to use the same strategy with every team. We found ways to save $20 million in postage and $16 million in adjustments *in a matter of hours*. We found ways to eliminate 8,000 unnecessary repair appointments a month, again in a matter of hours.

Sadly, in 1995, after five years of TQM, primarily focused on flowcharting processes not improving them, the leadership team shut down the quality department. Five years later, Qwest bought US West and in 18 months the stock went from $60 to $1 per share. Employment went from 70,000 to 30,000. A decade later, CenturyLink bought Qwest. I believe that our failure to solve the company's core business problems left it vulnerable to takeover and ultimately its demise.

FREE, PERFECT AND NOW

I no longer say that quality is about getting better, faster and cheaper, because the paradigm has shifted. Google, Amazon and Apple have taught people that you can get whatever you want *free, perfect and now!* In the new environment, it's no longer good enough to be better, faster and cheaper.

WHEN DO YOU WANT IT?   NOW!

HOW DO YOU WANT IT?   PERFECT!

HOW MUCH DO YOU WANT TO PAY?   FREE!

I remember when I used to go to a brick-and-mortar bookstore to buy a book. If they didn't have it in stock, they would order it for me and I'd wait a week for delivery. Then Amazon made it possible to order the book online (now) and have it delivered overnight if necessary (now). In 2007, the book industry took a huge leap toward *now*: you can download any eBook to a Kindle, Nook, or iPad *immediately* and pay less than you would for printed copy of the book (cheaper, but not quite free).

Amazon understands America's obsession with *now* (saving time). Amazon and publishers understand that they can make as much money selling an eBook at a lower cost than they can if they print, store and ship a physical book. E-books eclipsed the sales of physical books in 2011. Digital books and entertainment are the new "Gold Rush." Amazon cut 2.5 hours off its order-to-ship time in the last couple of years.

The iPhone and Android phones make it possible to search the web and consume TV and audio media right now. Same is true of iPads and other tablets; and it's "free."

Internet bandwidth is doubling in speed and halving in cost *every nine months.* As Chris Anderson, author of *Free*, says: "When something halves in price each year, zero is inevitable!"

Now most people will say: "But everything can't be free!" True, but I say the new standard every business will be judged by is how close they can get to *free, perfect and now.* To do this companies need *fast, affordable and flawless execution.*

Unfortunately, the old trial-and-error, gut-feel approaches to improving performance are too slow and error-prone to deliver anything close to free, perfect and now. The only hope any business has is to adopt the methods and tools of Lean Six Sigma to simplify, streamline and optimize performance. Lean Six Sigma will not fix a company's inability to innovate, but it will ensure that any innovation is delivered in a fast, affordable and flawless manner.

Customers have changed. Customers are smarter than most businesses. They quickly figure out which restaurants, retail shops, plumbers or whatever are *fast, affordable and flawless*. Critical care centers have sprung up because hospital emergency departments, in spite of their name, are too slow, averaging four hours for each patient according to Press Ganey. This statistic *has not changed for a decade*. It's not that some hospitals aren't doing it faster and with better outcomes for patients; it's just that most are not.

Most service businesses haven't explored Lean Six Sigma because they think it only applies to manufacturing. Information technologies departments haven't explored it because they don't think it applies to their software artisans. Of course, this is just lazy humans hoping the storm of free, perfect and now will somehow pass them by.

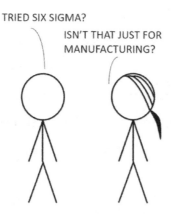

Lean Six Sigma can be applied anywhere to any business process. Anytime anything is produced or delivered, from a haircut to a jet engine, it's because people follow a process. It may be a fast, affordable, flawless process or a sluggish, error-prone costly one, but it's still a process. And Lean Six Sigma will simplify, streamline and optimize any process.

Unfortunately, Lean Six Sigma has its own problems. People think it costs too much, takes too long and is too complex. Based on how most people implement it, this is no surprise. Over half the time, it fails to put down roots or is plucked like a weed by a new CEO or leadership team.

UNSTOPPABLE LEAN SIX SIGMA

Lean Six Sigma can be fast, affordable and flawless, maximizing results while minimizing costs. To do so requires a fresh approach using what I call the Magnificent Seven Tools (more about these

11

tools later). Training doesn't have to take weeks or months; it can be done in a matter of hours. Projects don't have to take weeks or months to complete; I've done million-dollar projects in five days or less. The actual analysis can be done in under four hours, but sometimes implementation can take longer because it has to go through some sluggish, error-prone process (software enhancements for example).

Now some people will ask why everyone seems to be using the traditional Lean Six Sigma implementation approach. Are they all wrong? I say, not all, but most service businesses are headed for disappointment. Traditional Six Sigma training is designed to teach you everything you need to know to improve a *manufacturing plant's factory floor*. Since only one person in 100 works on a factory floor, those are the people who need the traditional approach. The other 99 out of 100 don't need all that stuff and it creates confusion, not results.

You can spend a lot of time and money training a lot of multicolored "belts," start teams that flounder and wonder what went wrong. Don't let this happen to you.

There is a better way, but you have to be willing to ease into it rather than jump into it. You have to be willing to narrow your focus, because performance problems aren't spread evenly over the company like butter on bread; they cluster in a few activities and gaps. To narrow your focus, you have to be willing to *reduce the number of people involved*. That's right, to accelerate adoption of Lean Six Sigma and increase results, you will want to reduce the number of people involved. No more wall-to-wall, floor-to-ceiling implementations. Lean Six Sigma needs teams laser-focused on solving core problems using data.

No one needs yet another jargon-ridden, statistical recipe book on how to bake Lean Six Sigma into a corporate culture. It doesn't work because cultures aren't cakes. Cultures are more like a herd of bison or a school of fish always moving and shifting, sometimes slowly, sometimes quickly. We need a way to nudge the culture toward excellence that doesn't invite a charge from the bulls or trigger a stampede.

Companies don't need more Green Belts or Black Belts. They need more *Money Belts*—people who can quickly find ways to save time and money to boost productivity and profitability. They have to learn how to eliminate the Three Silent Killers of productivity and profitability: **Delay, Defects** and **Deviation**. When they eliminate the delays, it makes the product or service available *now*. When they eliminate defects and deviation, products and services become *perfect*. Eliminating defects and deviation reduces costs so that products and services become more *affordable, even free*.

13

Agile Process Innovation will focus on the Magnificent Seven "Money Belt" Tools necessary to achieve stunning, breakthrough results. Master these and you can then add other methods and tools as required. As you improve, you'll begin to see opportunities to *innovate.*

Eliminate delay, defects and deviation, and your business will experience a quantum leap toward *free, perfect and now.* To do so you don't need long, expensive training or endless team meetings. You need 4-hour Money Belts focused on the most critical problems to start getting results immediately. It won't take long for customers to notice the improvement.

My Story

I took a couple of programming courses in college and computer software has been the focus of my life ever since. I've written and maintained software for mainframes, minicomputers and microcomputers (e.g., QI Macros®). I've used methodologies from Structured Programming to Waterfall to inventing my own (Rapid Evolutionary Development) which is an early version of what would become Agile. I've been doing "Agile" software development most of my adult life.

I know how to *build* error-prone software slowly and how to *grow* robust software quickly. By bridging my understanding of Agile software development and quality improvement, I've come to an approach I call *Agile Process Innovation*.

I've been involved with quality since 1990, long before Six Sigma became popular and right at the beginning of awareness of the Toyota Production System (TPS – a.k.a. Lean). My goal has been to spread the 'gospel' of quality and to create 100 Million Money Belts worldwide. This is a challenge because most people are afraid of math and statistics.

What if you could automate the math, statistics and much of Lean Six Sigma's analysis with software such as QI Macros? Could you shortcut everyone's learning experience? Could you help them achieve results in minutes or hours instead of months and years?

As the author of the QI Macros, *Lean Six Sigma Demystified* and *Lean Six Sigma for Hospitals*, I sit at a strange crossroads. I talk with many people who have been trained in Six Sigma but *have never done a project*. I find this wildly disappointing. If employees have been trained, but never done a project, I'd have to consider their training to have been a *waste* of time and money; it's a form of *overproduction*— one of the speed bumps of Lean.

I'm equally disappointed when employees finally try to apply Lean Six Sigma, that they are often confused about where to start. Their training covered so many methods and tools (overproduction) that they aren't sure what to do first. And this confusion stems from Six Sigma's roots in manufacturing.

While the U.S. manufacturing is still a two trillion-dollar business, manufacturing employment has been shrinking...shrinking to the point that only one employee out of every 100 needs all of the tools in Lean Six Sigma. The other 99 only need a few tools to solve most service-oriented operational problems.

The Long Tail of Tools

Lean Six Sigma training covers what I call the "long tail" of improvement methods and tools. This includes every tool you might ever need if you work in manufacturing. But they are overkill when starting the Six Sigma journey. And Black Belts freely admit that when faced with a more complex problem, they often have to look up what to do because they've forgotten everything from their training.

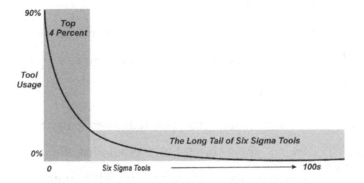

Solution: Let's get back to the fundamentals. What few key tools does a person need to know to solve most operational problems? What are the fundamentals?

> *"Whenever I read a 'simple' recipe, my first question is can I use half the ingredients and half the steps and get something people will not just love, but perhaps even prefer?"*
>
> -Timothy Ferriss – author of The 4-Hour Chef

In my 20+ years of improvement projects, I have found that a few key tools used in the right order can help companies save millions of dollars, cut costs, boost profits, boost productivity and even save lives. I've had months of quality training on everything from TQM to DOE, yet I have found that the Magnificent Seven Tools diagnose and treat almost everything. And when I occasionally do need to add another tool, there are plenty of examples and insights that are only a Google away.

In other words, you don't need to know everything to start getting results. You don't need months of training to start solving problems. You don't need to know formulas, decision trees or a lot of jargon. You just need to know a handful of tools, use software to create them and apply them to start getting results immediately.

Tim Ferriss and The 4-Hour Chef

Tim Ferriss, author of *The 4-Hour Workweek*, *The 4-Hour Body* and *The 4-Hour Chef,* is obsessed with accelerated learning and, as far as I can tell, wants to learn *everything.* The first chapter of *The 4-Hour Chef* is about "meta learning" – learning how to learn fast, because, he says, "Speed of learning determines value." And this is one of the problems with Lean Six Sigma training—it's too slow.

> *Two skills—fast learning and clear thinking are the key to 21st-century personal skills.*
>
> - Colin Rose and Malcolm J. Nichol- Accelerated Learning for the 21st Century.

Reading Ferriss' book led me to examine my own approach to helping people grasp Lean Six Sigma.

My Quality Journey

In the early 1990s, I attended a four-day workshop with W. Edwards Deming. While it was great to see the grand master in action, my "trainer" mind was thinking that if he'd used some accelerated learning techniques, we could have covered the same ground in *one day with greater comprehension.*

In 1990, when our five-day training classes with big 3-ring binders failed to produce successful teams and results, I started applying Six Sigma to itself. I applied everything I know about accelerated learning to Six Sigma, and later, Lean. I quickly reduced my classes to a one-day workshop.

I used to spend time teaching participants how to choose the right control chart, but I found that I could build these decisions into the QI Macros software. I found that with the QI Macros Wizards— Chart, Control Chart, Data Mining, PivotTable and Statistics— almost anyone could start drawing charts and solving problems immediately.

I found that when I teach the tools in the proper sequence: 1) control chart, 2) Pareto chart, 3) fishbone, and have participants practice immediately using test data provided with the QI Macros, they *skip over their fear of statistics*. Then I have them jump into analyzing their own data. There's nothing more satisfying than getting participants to analyze their own data and start doing root cause analysis and solving seemingly unsolvable problems *right in the classroom*. One company I trained found $90,000 in savings that afternoon. You can too.

> *The tools of learning are not fixed, nor is the amount of time needed to become world-class.*
>
> – Timothy Ferriss

I teach Lean *complete with value stream maps, spaghetti diagrams and action plans to simplify and streamline key processes immediately* in less than four hours. And I teach Six *Sigma while delivering projects ready for root cause analysis or implementation* in less than four hours. In one day, my students leave the classroom knowing more about Six Sigma than I knew after weeks of excellent training in 1990.

So, can you learn to be instantly productive with Six Sigma in four hours? Yes, I believe you can. Will you know everything in the Six Sigma body of knowledge (BOK)? Not a chance, but this way you can start solving the most common types of problems immediately and then add methods and tools as needed.

Will you be instantly proficient? No, but who is? It can take one-to-two years and $250,000 to bring a Black Belt fully up to speed. By applying the Magnificent Seven Tools for only a few hours every week using QI Macros, you'll be able to move your department or company from 3-sigma to 5-sigma in 18-24 months. You'll start solving seemingly *unsolvable* problems in a matter of hours.

4-Hour Lean Six Sigma Training

> *It is possible to vastly compress most learning.* –
>
> Timothy Ferriss

To make these 4-hour training sessions easily accessible and affordable, I've put my Agile Lean Six Sigma Yellow Belt training online, *for free*, at www.lssyb.com. I call it "Money Belt" training, because it focuses on using the key tools to save time and money while boosting productivity and profitability. Now *anyone* can learn to be a Money Belt.

Certification

> *People learn from projects, not training.*
>
> -Ken Norton – author of We Don't Make Widgets

Sadly, I have found that many people only want a Green Belt or Black Belt certification to enhance their resume, not their company. Many certification programs do not require an improvement project to demonstrate competency. Most certification programs do not provide the student with Six Sigma software (e.g., QI Macros®).

21

I think that finding ways to make a business faster, better, cheaper and safer is a lot of fun. It's a skill you can use forever, wherever you work. It will spill over into your personal life, leaving you more time for family and friends. And it will leave the world a better place. But hey, it's up to you. Haven't you waited long enough to start learning Agile Process Innovation?

Jay Arthur

Denver, CO

June 2019

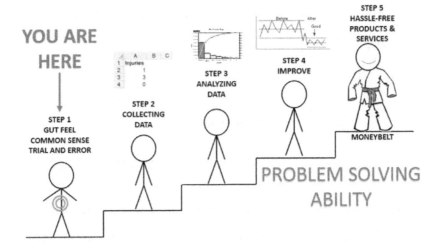

IF YOU DON'T HAVE THE TIME TO READ THIS BOOK, HERE'S WHAT IT SAYS:

Lean Six Sigma, as it is traditionally implemented, takes too long, costs too much and often fails to deliver the expected results. Instead of 160 hours over four months, *you can learn the core skills and start making improvements in four hours or less.* You don't need to know everything to do anything; you only need to know how to use a handful of tools in the proper sequence to start getting results immediately. This is what I call *Agile Process Innovation.*

The future belongs to companies whose "Money Belts" can use these tools to maximize productivity and profits while minimizing costs.

Questions this book answers:

4. What is Agile Process Innovation?

5. Why do we need it now?

6. Why is it foolish to spend two-to-four weeks learning Lean Six Sigma when you can do it in eight hours or less?

7. What are the key tools you need to solve 99% of all business problems?

8. How can every business, large and small, service and manufacturing use the methods and tools of Lean Six Sigma to start achieving breakthroughs in speed, quality and profitability quickly and at low cost?

> *Choose the highest-yield material and you can be an idiot and enjoy stunning success.*
>
> –Timothy Ferriss – Author of the 4-Hour Chef

Yes, this book is short, because if it's short, it's more likely to be used and because I believe that you don't need to know everything about Lean Six Sigma to start getting results, process improvements and process innovations. Unless you work on a manufacturing factory floor, there's a limit to how much is *useful* to learn.

AGILE PROCESS INNOVATION

Over time, every business process becomes increasingly complicated. Exceptions, workarounds and all manner of process tweaks turn simple processes into complex, unmanageable ones.

In the 1990s, I was assigned to a team attempting to "reengineer" the phone company's billing computer system and processes. This system had evolved over decades so it knew more about how we invoiced customers that anyone could possibly redesign. After several years and tens of millions of dollars, the project was shelved.

WHERE DO I START?

FIX THE WORST FIRST

Meanwhile, I worked with teams that figured out how to save $20 million in postage costs by redesigning the bill (not the whole billing system). We saved $16 million in adjustments. By attacking the most expensive and problematic portions of the billing system, we found ways to make breakthrough improvements while the reengineering effort was grinding toward failure.

Reengineering became a popular movement to improve business operations. Reengineering presupposed that business is a "machine" that could be redesigned. Attempting to reengineer an entire business process usually came with a high cost and catastrophic results because businesses aren't machines. Businesses are more like a living system—people, processes and technology working in harmony to serve customers.

I have found that improving processes to simplify, streamline and optimize performance leads to insights about how to redesign the process. *Process innovations grow out of improvements.*

To achieve Agile Process Innovation, you will want both: improvement and innovation.

The tools of quality improvement have been around for almost 100 years. Whether you call it TQM, Six Sigma, Lean, Operational Excellence or something else, I think we have to wonder why the tools of quality aren't in every business worldwide. My theory: the quality community has made improvement too complicated.

In today's economy, people don't have time to learn complicated methodologies and technologies. Smart phones have taught them that complicated things can be simplified and learned quickly. People often ask: "Is there an app for that?"

With all of the progress made in software for smart phones, websites and so on, why is Lean Six Sigma still taught in the slow, methodical way it was taught in the 1990s?

An October 2016 Harvard Business Review article calls this "The Great Training Robbery." The authors say, "For the most part, the learning doesn't lead to better organizational performance, because people soon revert to their old ways of doing things." One study found that, "Companies that tried to launch major transformations by training hundreds of thousands of employees across many units lagged behind the companies that didn't kick-start their transformation this way."

Sounds like the traditional method of implementing Six Sigma, doesn't it? Lots of training, *before* results.

More recently, the Editor-in-Chief of Harvard Business Review said: "Corporate survival today requires the capacity for rapid change and forward-thinking. HR departments are taking their cues from a surprising source—the IT department, which at many organizations has adopted agile processes to speed its evolution and better serve customer needs." The article, *HR Goes Agile*, references a 2017 Deloitte survey in which 79% of global executive rated agile performance management as a high organizational priority. If today's executives expect *Agile* (think: voice of the customer), then why aren't we delivering it?

> *Whenever you find yourself on the side of the majority, it is time to pause and reflect. —*
>
> Mark Twain

The writing is on the wall—Lean Six Sigma needs to *pivot* to a new way of achieving desired results. Integrating Agile into Lean Six Sigma is an easy way to do it.

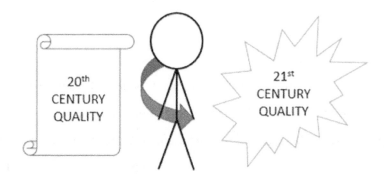

What is Agile? A method that "is characterized by the division of tasks into short phrases of work and frequent reassessment and adaptation of plans." Agile focuses on speed and adaptability, not rigid adherence to archaic methods.

Innovative process transformations emerge from simplifying, streamlining and optimizing key processes using the Magnificent Seven Tools of Lean Six Sigma (described in a later chapter). I would like you to consider that any attempt to "reengineer" a complex business process will fail without this prework.

AGILE LEAN SIX SIGMA

The January-February 2017 Harvard Business Review article on problem solving found that 85% of C-suite executives say their companies struggle with *problem diagnosis,* not problem solving, and that this comes with a significant cost. (Joseph Juran often said that companies spend 25-33% of costs on waste and rework. This is the hidden cost of problems.) *Six Sigma is too complex and time-consuming to fit into a regular workday,* says author, Thomas Wedell-Wedellsborg. *We need tools that don't require the entire organization to undergo weeks-long training programs.*

I'd like you to consider that the Six Sigma body of knowledge and training was designed for improving a manufacturing plant—20th Century quality. That's why we need a simplified and streamlined, 21st Century approach to Lean Six Sigma that fits *services*, because that's where the jobs are.

Origins of Agile

For many decades, the method of software development was called *Waterfall* development. It took too long and often failed to deliver the expected output. Then in 2000, a rogue group of programmers got together and applied the principles of Lean to software development. They came up with a fresh approach to software that they named *Agile*.

Consider that Agile grew out of Lean, so Lean Six Sigma can also benefit from Agile. Over the years I've applied Lean principles and techniques to both Lean and Six Sigma for service companies. The result is faster implementation with rapid results. Accelerating Lean Six Sigma improves productivity and profits and creates buzz.

The Agile programmers came up with a new set of values and objectives.

The Agile Values:

- **Individuals and interactions** over processes and tools
- **Working software** over comprehensive documentation

- **Customer collaboration** over contract negotiation
- **Responding to change** over following a plan
- **Numerous small experiments** over a few large bets
- **Testing and data** over opinions and habits (sounds like Six Sigma doesn't it?)
- **Engagement and transparency** over posturing

I believe that we can adapt these values to Lean Six Sigma:

The Agile Lean Six Sigma Values:

- **Results** over rigor

- **Working improvements** over comprehensive documentation

- **Cross-functional collaboration** over silo analysis

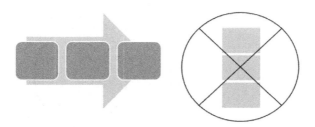

- **Responding to change** over following a plan

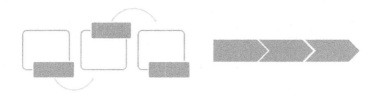

- **Numerous small experiments** over a few large bets

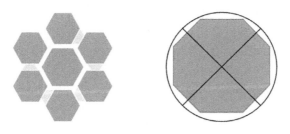

- **Testing, data and charts** over opinions and conventions

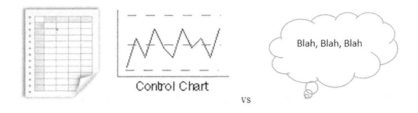

33

- **Engagement and transparency** over posturing

Lean Six Sigma Agile Manifesto

By changing one word, *software* to *improvement,* I believe we can also adapt the Agile Manifesto. The Lean Six Sigma Agile Manifesto is based on twelve principles:

1. **Satisfy customers** by early and continuous delivery of valuable *improvements*

2. **Welcome changing requirements**, even late in the *improvement*

3. **Deliver working *improvements*** frequently (in hours or days rather than weeks)

4. **Close, daily cooperation** between business people and *improvers*

5. **Build projects around motivated individuals**, who should be trusted

6. **Face-to-face conversation** is the best form of communication (co-location)

7. **Working *improvements*** are the primary measure of progress

8. **Sustainable *improvements*,** able to maintain a constant pace

9. **Continuous attention to technical excellence and good design**

10. **Simplicity**—the art of maximizing the amount of work *not done*—is essential

11. **Self-organizing teams** deliver the best architectures, requirements, and

12. **Regular team reflection** on how to become more effective and adjusts accordingly

Agile Lean Six Sigma Misconceptions

When trying to adjust to Agile Lean Six Sigma as a way of working, people often try to find excuses why it won't work. If you've spent a lot of time learning long-form Six Sigma, you will feel uncomfortable in a sprint. Here are some misconceptions:

- **Agile is a sloppy, ad-hoc approach to Lean Six Sigma.** If anything, it's an accelerated application of the methods and tools that starts with data and achieves results much more quickly.

- **Agile improvement isn't predictable.** Because Agile LSS restricts the methods and tools to seven key tools used on the most common types of business problems, it is much more predictable. It always delivers working improvements.

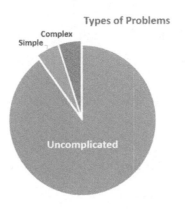

- **Agile improvements are hard to manage.** Since improvement teams only meet for a few hours to develop root causes and countermeasures, teams are easier to manage. Implementing the improvement is also easier to manage.

- **Agile LSS means no documentation.** Every project should consist of control charts, Pareto charts or histograms, fishbone diagrams, countermeasures and action plans. These are the minimum viable outputs of a project. Other tools can be used but may be unnecessary.

- **Agile Process Innovation is the solution to all of your problems.** No, Agile LSS is the solution to the most

36

common problems experienced by service businesses. Manufacturing plants may require Design of Experiments, Measurement Systems Analysis and other tools that are not needed in service businesses.

- **There is only one way to do Agile Process Innovation.** The Agile Process Innovation Manifesto lays out core values and principles. It does not say "how" to do it. I'm offering my version as a starting point: simplify, streamline, optimize and innovate (SSOI).

Hacking Lean Six Sigma

Is it possible to accelerate the adoption and use of Lean Six Sigma by hacking how it's implemented? By *hacking*, I mean the good kind of hacking (white hat not black hat)—simplifying, streamlining and optimizing the methods and tools to maximize results with minimal investment.

Hackers try to build the best services over the long term by quickly releasing and learning from smaller iterations rather than trying to get everything right all at once.

-Mark Zuckerberg – The Hacker Way

https://www.wired.com/2012/02/zuck-letter/)

The spirit of hacking [can] be adapted and applied to general business management, not just technical innovation. Scott Brinker – Hacking Marketing

---

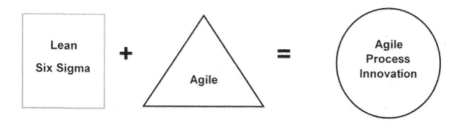

Modern performance improvement has a lot in common with software development.

Parallel Revolutions

- From rigid processes to agile

- From maintaining the status quo to accelerating speed and adaptability

- From big projects to evolving customer experiences

- From silos to engagement

- From complexity to simplicity

Hacking Lean

Is it possible to accelerate the adoption and use of Lean methods and tools by *hacking Lean*? I believe the answer to this question is YES!

While Lean came from the world of manufacturing—the Toyota Production System (TPS)—80 percent of American businesses are service businesses. Can these businesses use a subset of Lean to maximize performance? Yes, again.

We now live in a digital world. The key characteristics of the digital world, according to Scott Brinker, author of *Hacking Marketing* are speed and adaptability. Brinker says the challenges in a digital world are:

1. How do we execute faster?

2. How do we resist unwise knee-jerk reactions or overheated churn?

If you look at Lean Six Sigma training, it is essentially unchanged for decades. I believe that this model no longer serves U.S. service businesses and slows the tempo of change.

In manufacturing companies, most of the unnecessary delays and movement have been eliminated from the factory floor. But in service companies, delays *between* processing steps represent the vast majority of performance problems. To eliminate unnecessary delays, employees only need two tools: value stream mapping and spaghetti diagramming to redesign process flow and movement.

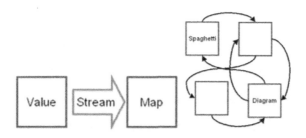

That's it! That's all you need to start hacking Lean in a service environment. Joseph Juran talked about the "Vital few, trivial many." It applies to methods and tools as well as improvements.

Because **most service delays occur in the arrows between steps**, you don't need to know TAKT time, change over time or anything about optimizing the *steps* until you eliminate the delays *between* steps. That's how we hack Lean for services.

Lean Sprints

The week-long Kaizen blitz is a thing of the past unless you work someplace where you can shut down for five days. You just can't shut down a nursing unit for a week. You have to transform the unit in operation. This suggests the need for an *agile* approach to improvement. In other words, a *sprint*.

Using a one-to-two hour *timebox*, focus on one element of improvement at a time. A series of these small bets will find the best solution more quickly.

All you need are a pad of Post-it® Notes and a flipchart to map the process flow or movement. This can be done in less than an hour. Once you know the current state, you can design a desired state that eliminates delay and movement. This can also be done in less than an hour. Then it's just a matter of changing procedures and layouts to achieve the desired state. Some can be done immediately; some may take a while.

In an hour or less, I've seen nurses redesign a nursing unit in ways that reduce nurse travel by 50 percent or more. This means more time with patients, better patient outcomes, better patient satisfaction and better nursing satisfaction.

In an hour or two, I've seen a computer operation group rethink nightly batch processing and reduce the cycle time from nine hours to one.

Eliminating unnecessary delays and movement will automatically reduce waste and rework because you eliminate the opportunity to miss a step or do a step twice. It may automatically reduce overproduction, inventory and non-value-added processing.

It doesn't matter what service you provide, there's always a way to reduce unnecessary delay and movement.

Hacking Six Sigma

Is it possible to accelerate the adoption and use of Six Sigma methods and tools by *hacking Six Sigma*? I believe the answer to this question is YES!

Traditional Lean Six Sigma implementations take months or even years to see results: months of training followed by projects that take months to complete. This is the traditional method of implementing Lean Six Sigma, but not the best way.

Traditional Lean Six Sigma

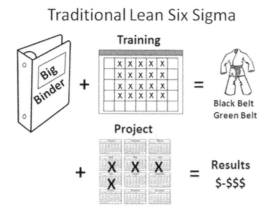

Agile Lean Six Sigma training takes a different approach.

Using existing data and QI Macros, we can train employees in a day or less *and* solve real problems:

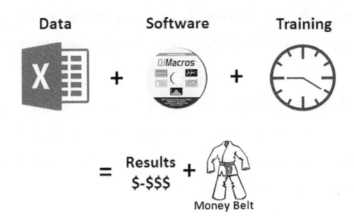

> *Hacking is the art of invention. – Scott Brinker*
>
> *Hacking just means building something quickly or testing the boundaries of what can be done.*
>
> -Mark Zuckerberg – *The Hacker Way*

Recommendation: Stop managing for activities (number of teams started) and start managing for outcomes (bottom-line, profit-enhancing results).

Vital Few, Trivial Many

A handful of tools will solve most business problems, especially in service industries:

- PivotTables – to analyze raw data and find the *invisible low-hanging fruit*

PivotTable

- Control Charts – XmR chart of defect rates or cycle times. Dr. Donald Wheeler calls the XmR Chart the *Swiss Army Knife* of control charts.

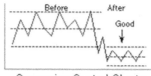

Comparing Control Charts

- Pareto Charts – Types of defects

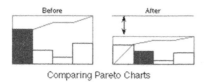

Comparing Pareto Charts

- Histograms – cycle (turnaround) times

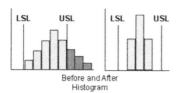

Before and After
Histogram

- Fishbone (Ishikawa) Diagrams – root cause analysis

Cause-Effect Diagram

- Countermeasures and Action Plans (Matrices)

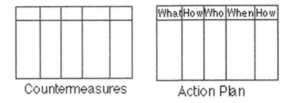

Countermeasures   Action Plan

These tools will diagnose and solve the vast majority of operational problems. Are there more *complex* problems that need more exotic tools? Of course there are, but first solve all of the *less complicated* problems.

Agile Principles

Under an agile business management model, agile techniques, practices, principles and values are expressed across five domains:

1. **Cross-functional engagement** – to embed customers and suppliers within any project process to share accountability for product/service improvement.

46

2. **Facilitation-based management** – adopting agile management models to facilitate the day-to-day operation of teams.

3. **Agile work practices** – adopting specific iterative and incremental work practices.

4. **An enabling organizational structure** – with a focus on staff engagement, personal autonomy and outcomes-based governance.

5. **An education model** that blends agile practices and philosophies to create micro-schools that emphasize collaborative culture creation and self-directed learning.

Benefits of Agile Lean Six Sigma

1. Better improvements

2. Higher satisfaction

3. Higher team morale

4. Increased collaboration and ownership

5. More relevant metrics

6. Improved performance

7. Improved project predictability

Agile Metrics

- Sprint success rates – LSS *velocity*

- Defects and turnaround times

- Total project duration

- Time to implement

- Total project cost

- ROI

How to Hack the Lean Six Sigma Learning Curve

Have you ever tried to learn something one way and found it too hard, but then you tried another way and it was easy? I grew up in Tucson, Arizona in the heart of the Sonoran Desert. When I moved to Denver, my coworkers hauled me up to the ski slopes, helped me rent 5.5-foot skis and sent me off to the bunny hill for lessons. The instructors used the *snowplow* method to teach us how to ski—you shape the skis into an inverted V and bend your knees in to carve a turn. I couldn't get it.

A couple of years later, the ski club at Bell Labs invited me up to Vermont with the promise of a magical new way to learn to ski called *graduated-length* method. I started at 9am on 3.5 ft. skis. Graduated to 4.5 ft. skis by lunch. Moved up to 5.5 ft. skis the next morning. *I went from zero to hero in 24 hours.* On Maui, I learned how to play ukulele in *one-hour* from Jason Jerome at Lahaina Music.

Can we do the same thing with Lean Six Sigma?

How do we solve the Six Sigma learning problem?

- First, remove everything that is purely manufacturing focused (e.g., hypothesis testing, DOE, etc.) because over 80% of U.S. employees work in service industries.

- Second, eliminate formulas and manual calculations. Six Sigma trainers forget that most people are *terrified* of math and statistics. Let QI Macros do the math and statistics. Let people analyze the resulting insights and charts, then make improvements.

- Automate everything that can be automated.

How to Hack DMAIC Project Development and Selection

I'm about to propose a solution you might consider a shameless plug, but it's in keeping with Toyota's concept of autonomation—automation with the human touch. We can solve Six Sigma implementation delays by letting software (e.g., QI Macros) do the heavy lifting. Feel free to use any other Six Sigma software you prefer, but I have tweaked QI Macros to eliminate the learning curve and get people to actionable improvement stories in minutes, not weeks, months or years. No other software can do what QI Macros does.

Problem: Most Six Sigma Training spends at least three days on the methods and tools of Define, Measure and Analyze. When you spread the training out over multiple days, it makes Six Sigma seem slow and cumbersome.

Solution: Use the QI Macros Data Mining Wizard on Raw Data to Create Projects

- One minute of Data Mining Wizard will turn raw data into the PivotTables, control charts, Pareto charts and fishbones required for root cause analysis. Yes—QI Macros Data Mining Wizard can create entire improvement projects, ready for analysis, in *seconds!*

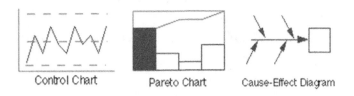

Control Chart   Pareto Chart   Cause-Effect Diagram

- Two hours of understanding the output and selecting projects

How to Collapse Control Chart Training

Problem: Five-day Control Chart classes focus on manually calculating the formulas and drawing XmR, XbarR, XbarS, c, np, p, u charts. There is no reason to do this manually. I used to spend hours teaching people how to navigate a control chart decision tree, but people don't naturally think in decision trees. In 2006 I figured out how to automate the control chart decision tree in QI Macros.

Problem solved!

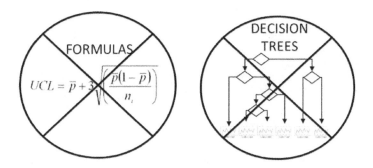

Solution: Use the QI Macros Control Chart Wizard to select the right chart automatically.

- One minute using QI Macros Control Chart Wizard to create a control chart.

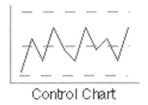
Control Chart

- Two hours of *understanding the patterns* in control charts:

51

o Special Causes – out-of-control points that should only occur 3 times out of 1000

o Common Causes – variation

o Outcomes: 1) move the center line up or down, 2) reduce variation.

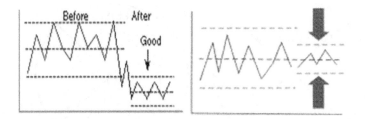

Once people understand the patterns they are looking for and the outcomes to be achieved, they quickly orient themselves to figuring out how to *win the game*.

How to Collapse Capability Analysis

Problem: Capability Analysis training focuses on manually drawing histograms and calculating Cp, Cpk, Pp and Ppk. This is slow, confusing and unnecessary.

Solution: Use QI Macros Histogram or Capability Suite

- One minute to create a histogram or Capability Suite consisting of a control chart, histogram, normal probability plot and so on.

- Two hours of *understanding the patterns* in histograms:

    o Capable (Cp>1, Cpk>1) vs Not Capable (Cp<1, Cpk<1)

    o Outcomes: 1) center the data, 2) reduce variation.

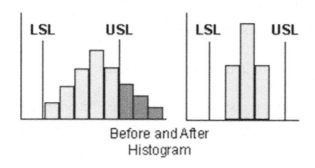

Before and After
Histogram

Again, once people understand the desired transformation, they will figure out how to win the game.

    o Consider using Weibull histogram for non-normal data if needed.

How to Collapse Hypothesis Testing

Problem: Hypothesis testing mainly focuses on comparing central tendency and variation. This takes a day or more. Honestly, I've never used hypothesis testing because I don't work in manufacturing or research. I work on achieving business results: speed, quality and profitability.

Solution: Eliminate Hypothesis Testing all together. Stop trying to turn people into statisticians. If you must teach hypothesis testing, use the QI Macros Stat Wizard.

- One minute of Stat Wizard will do t-tests, F-tests, ANOVA, or Levenes test on sample data.

- One hour of understanding the results:

  o Forget the statistical jargon (e.g., "cannot reject the null hypothesis"). Stop trying to teach normal people to speak like statisticians. Focus on results:

    ▪ Means are the same or different
    ▪ Variation is the same or different
    ▪ What to do in either case

Non-Normal Data

Problem: People agonize over what kind of data they have and what to do with it.

Solution: Don't cover non-normal data. Control charts are robust to non-normal data. Service turnaround times are often non-normal, but the goal is to reduce variation and move the average. Agonizing over normality will not simplify the analysis.

Team Dynamics

Problem: Most Six Sigma training includes topics like brainstorming, multivoting, team dynamics (form, storm, norm, perform), etc. I have found that given a meaningful project to work on, teams will jump into action.

Solution: *Let the data pick the project.* Teams should *never brainstorm what problem to solve, because they usually want to fix someone else—customers, suppliers, management or subordinates.* Instead, use the Data Mining Wizard to analyze raw data. Then select team members based on the results of the data analysis. The team will self-organize to solve the problems revealed. Only teach specific methods when they are needed for a real project.

Measurement Systems Analysis (MSA),

Problem: Most Six Sigma courses teach MSA, GageR&R, Design of Experiments (DOE) and other complex tools used only on manufacturing factory floors.

Solution: Don't teach these methods to service companies, because it's a waste of time and causes confusion. It's a form of *overproduction*, which violates a basic rule of Lean.

Six Sigma History

Problem: Most Six Sigma courses teach the history of Six Sigma from Shewhart, Juran and Deming to the present. This is also a non-value-added waste of time.

Solution: Point people to excellent online references about this *if they want to know the history*. People don't need to know the origins of quality; they want to know the *future* of quality.

Comparing Lean Six Sigma Bodies of Knowledge

I took the ASQ LSS Yellow Belt Body of Knowledge (BOK) and stripped out everything *not* required to solve problems in a service environment. The word count dropped from 1281 words to 144, an 89% reduction. Think of it as using *5S* on Lean Six Sigma.

I believe that Agile LSS Yellow Belt training is all that is required to solve the vast majority of problems facing American business. Anything else is overkill and problematic.

I did the same thing with the LSS Green Belt BOK. The word count fell from 3133 to 2178; a 30% reduction. I think GB and BB trainings are ideal for people who work on a manufacturing factory floor that represents less than 2% of the workforce. About 2% work in agriculture. Everyone else works in services. Most of the people employed in manufacturing work in the service side of the business:

sales, marketing, ordering, invoicing, purchasing and customer service. They only need Agile Money Belt tools.

When I went to college to study systems engineering, I learned operations research, differential equations and all kinds of stuff that I might need. *I have never used any of it.* Similarly, teaching service employees how to improve a factory is a foolish waste of time, money and resources.

If we can get people using QI Macros to solve problems immediately using real data, they will embrace Lean Six Sigma and accelerate the quality transformation. So far, I have seen only limited signs of real improvement across many industries. Why not?

I believe it's because we're still trying to teach Six Sigma the same way it has been done for the last two decades to prepare people for non-existent jobs in manufacturing. Most Six Sigma software is cumbersome and doesn't help analyze data, select the right charts or statistics automatically. QI Macros simplifies, streamlines and optimizes the learning experience. I routinely take people from zero to hero in one day using QI Macros.

We can cling to our traditions or embrace a new and improved way to engage people in problem solving that gets results. I believe it's time for *Agile Lean Six Sigma.*

THE MAGNIFICENT SEVEN TOOLS OF LEAN SIX SIGMA

The 1960s film, *The Magnificent Seven*, starred Yul Brenner, Steve McQueen, Charles Bronson, James Coburn, Robert Vaughn, Brad Dexter and Horst Buckholz. These seven hired gunmen protect a Mexican village from the bandit Calvera played by Eli Wallach. The film was an Americanization of the Japanese film *The Seven Samurai*. The film implies that you don't need an army to win the war, just seven top "gun men."

The Magnificent Seven of Lean Six Sigma

> *Becoming a master of karate was not about learning 4,000 moves but about doing just a handful of moves 4,000 times.* — Chet Holmes

Over the years, in project after project, I have found myself returning to the same Magnificent Seven Tools:

	The Magnificent Seven	
1		**Process Mapping Tools:** **Value Stream Maps** to identify and **remove delays** in any process. **Spaghetti Diagrams** to identify and **eliminate unnecessary movement** of people or materials.
2	PivotTable	**Excel PivotTables** to summarize defect data. Every million-dollar improvement project I've ever worked on began with PivotTables.
3	Control Chart	**Control Charts** to measure and monitor the performance of any process. I have found that no one can sustain an

		improvement *without control charts.*
4	Pareto Chart	**Pareto Charts** to identify the most common types of defects. Pareto charts are my go-to chart for pinpointing problems and solutions.
5	LSL USL Histogram	**Histograms** to evaluate *deviation* in process performance. I use these in service industries to analyze turnaround times (e.g., hospital wait times, lab turnaround times, etc.)

| 6 | Cause-Effect Diagram | **Ishikawa diagrams** to document the root causes of each "big bar" on the Pareto chart or out-of-spec products on the histogram. |
| 7 | Checksheet

Countermeasures   Action Plan | **Matrix diagrams** like check sheets, countermeasures and action plans to collect data and prioritize corrective actions.

Sometimes we collect data manually using a check sheet to get a quick read on a problem area. |

I have found that these seven tools can help teams solve 99% of the problems facing a typical business. Sure, you will need more exotic tools to solve problems in the last one percent, but you won't need them for a while, maybe a long while.

Are you stuck trying to figure out what tools to use in what order? Try the Magnificent Seven to deliver breakthrough improvements. You'll be surprised how far you can go with just these tools.

> *The unexamined process becomes sluggish and error-prone.* —
>
> Jay Arthur

If you have preventable:

- **Delays** – use value stream maps and spaghetti diagrams to evaluate the work flow and remove delay.

- **Defects** – use PivotTables, control charts, Pareto charts and Fishbone diagrams (QI Macros Data Mining Wizard) to pinpoint and fix the root causes of defects.

- **Deviation** – use control charts, histograms and Fishbone diagrams to pinpoint and eliminate the root causes of variation

THE 4-HOUR LEAN HACK

Agile is Lean applied to software development. I wrote a book about a similar methodology called Rapid Evolutionary Development back in 1989. Both are about rapid iteration to converge on a deliverable solution when "the problem is complicated, solutions are initially unknown and product requirements will most likely change."

In many ways, *Agile* is like the Lean Startup methodology: Build, Measure, Learn. We also find it in the OODA Loop (observe, orient, decide, act) developed by fighter pilot John Boyd. "Thinking about operating at a quicker tempo…engaging in activity that is so quick it is disorienting [and] inhibits the adversary's ability to adapt. Whoever can handle the quickest rate of change is the one who survives." Even *Systems Thinking* argued that the company that learns faster than its competition wins. From these and other sources I think we can begin to consider that rapid learning, faster iteration and rapid prototyping are the key to *blitzscaling* a company's performance. Agile approaches to management have begun to spill over from IT into adjacent customer and management arenas.

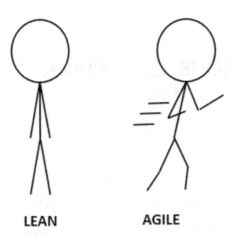

LEAN   **AGILE**

Agile sounds more desirable than Lean, doesn't it? Would you rather be agile or lean? Maybe this is a new way to approach implementing Lean or the Toyota Production System in a company. Rather than wall-to-wall, floor-to-ceiling implementations of Lean, start in IT and let the methods spill over into neighboring work units until it reaches a critical mass.

This is how cultures adopt, adapt or reject change. It might be worth a try

Nike's slogan is "Just Do It!" For businesses, the new slogan is "Just Do It NOW!" Customers no longer want to wait for anything if they know it's possible to get it right now. So, every business has two choices: 1) figure out how to deliver the product or service immediately or 2) wait for someone else to figure out how to *just do it now* and put you out of business. It only takes about four hours to start getting results.

Fortunately, Lean has figured out how to simplify and streamline any business process to make it lightning fast. There's a simple acronym that covers the speed bumps of Lean that inhibit a company's ability to *just do it now*—DOWNTIME:

- **D**elay – Unnecessary delays between steps in a process

- **O**verproduction – making stuff that no customer has ordered

- **W**aste and Rework – caused by mistakes, errors, defects and deviation

- **N**on-value-added (NVA) processing (e.g., inspection and rework)

- **T**ransportation – unnecessary movement of materials

- **I**nventory – unnecessary raw materials, work in process (WIP) or finished goods

- **M**otion – unnecessary movement of employees

- **E**mployee creativity – unused wisdom of the workers

While most manufacturing companies have figured out how to optimize the production line using these tools, the vast majority of service companies are barely aware of how to simplify and streamline business operations. Based on my experience in all kinds of industries from healthcare to telecom to IT to manufacturing, a couple of key tools will slash the time it takes to do anything.

Delay

In most service businesses and the "back room" functions of all businesses (orders, invoicing, purchasing, payments, HR, IT, etc.), *unnecessary delays between steps* (i.e., *arrows*) are the main cause of sluggish performance. Most business processes grow up in an ad-hoc fashion over time. To deal with inconsistencies, they develop too many workarounds and rework loops. They become *Frankenprocesses*. They suffer from too many *unnecessary* delays between steps.

When most people look at a process flow, they see a flowchart that looks like this:

I see something very different, huge delays and piles of unfinished work products—work in process (i.e., inventory):

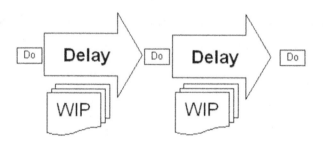

There's very little actual "doing" in most processes and a whole lot of delay (i.e., waiting around). And most business processes do

3-57 Rule

People Working
3 Minutes

57 Minutes
Delay

things in *big batches* so that there is always *work in process* (WIP) waiting for the next step in its development. Big batches supposedly create economies of scale, but all they do is create opportunities for mistakes, errors and additional delays.

This leads us to a few simple rules (adapted from Stalk and Hout's book, *Competing Against Time*):

The 3-57 Rule: In most businesses, employees are only working on the product or service for 3 minutes out of every hour, leaving 57 minutes of delay. To this most managers will say: "But my people are busy!" Yes they are, but the *thing* going through the process is not. It's idle 95 percent of the time—57 minutes per hour. Don't believe me? Start with any customer's order and follow it around. Bring a novel to pass the time.

The Dark Side of the 3-57 Rule: *Trying to make people faster is a waste of time,* because employees only account for 3 minutes out of every 60. Even if you make your people twice as fast, you'll only save 1.5 minutes per hour. You have to *make your lazy product faster* by eliminating the delays between processing steps.

> *Trying to make employees faster will only save a minute or two out of every hour of elapsed time.* -Jay Arthur

The 15-2-20 Rule: For every 15 minutes per hour you reduce those 57 minutes of delay, you will *double productivity and increase profit margins by 20 percent.* Since it's usually easy to eliminate these delays, it's possible to boost productivity two-four-eight-fold and profit margins by 20-40-80-100 percent. With Lean tools it's easy to do this quickly.

The Dark Side of the 15-2-20 Rule: Every *increase* in delay *decreases* productivity and profitability. Example: approvals required before doing anything.

The 3x2 Rule: Reducing delays will enable any business to grow three times faster than their competition and double productivity.

The Dark Side of the 3x2 Rule: If you don't get faster, your competitors will.

How do we achieve these breakthrough reductions in delay?

15-2-20 Rule

15 Minutes =
20% Profit

11 12 1

10   2

              3
57 Minutes

8   Delay   4

7   6   5

At the heart of every difficult decision lie three tough choices: What to pursue versus what to ignore. What to leave in versus what to leave out. What to do versus what to don't. The key is to remove the stupid stuff: anything obviously excessive, confusing, wasteful, unnatural, hazardous, hard to use or ugly. **This is the art of subtraction.** – Matthew E May

First, Simplify the Workspace

Any workspace collects clutter. The "5S" process is like spring cleaning. Just get a small team to spend a few hours to:

- **Sort** the needed from the unneeded (e.g., outdated forms, unused machines and materials, etc.). Dispose of the unneeded stuff.

- **Straighten** by making everything *visual and self-explanatory* (e.g., color-code things and label them).

- **Shine** – clean the workspace.

- **Standardize** the ongoing sorting, straightening and shining of the workspace.

- **Sustain** the simplification process by repeating every few months.

Once you've simplified the workspace using 5S, it's easy to redesign the workflow and workspace for optimal performance.

Then, Map the Value Stream to Reduce Delays

It's easy to eliminate delays. Simply flowchart or map the value stream. (Watch my video at www.qimacros.com/Moneybelt/lean-value-stream-map-patient-scheduling.html). Put times on each *arrow* of the process. You'll quickly discover that most of the cycle time is consumed *between* steps.

There are only two main ways to radically speed up a process:

- Redesign the process to eliminate delays.

- Redesign the process to do some steps in parallel.

You should be able to eliminate 80-90 percent of the overall cycle time which will boost productivity and profits by 50 percent or more.

Four-Hour Sprint: It only takes a handful of Post-it® Notes, a flipchart, a few subject-matter experts and a maximum of four hours to diagnose and redesign most processes for improved efficiency and effectiveness.

Then Spaghetti Diagram the Workspace to Reduce Movement

Again, using Post-its and a flipchart, a handful of employees can diagram the workspace and movement of employees, customers and materials through the space. If you're not sure how to do it, just follow a variety of customer orders around the office, factory, hospital or other facility. An aptly named "spaghetti diagram" will arise from this analysis.

www.qimacros.com/Moneybelt/lean-spaghetti-diagram.html

Simply rearrange processing "stations" to minimize movement of people and products. It's not unusual to reduce movement by 50 percent or more and slash cycle time.

Shift from Economies of Scale to Economies of Speed

One of the secrets of Toyota's Production System is called *one-piece flow*. The idea is to get down to a batch size of one, not 100 or 1000. When you can make one of anything immediately, you don't need any inventory. If Taco Bell can take a drive-through order, make a taco and a burrito, take payment and deliver the order in 180 seconds, why can't you do the same thing with whatever it is that you do?

What if you don't make anything? Sure you do. Every office worker produces forms. Service reps produce orders. Computers produce transactions (e.g., real-time vs batch).

Simply redesign the process to reduce batch sizes, ideally to a size of one. An exception to this rule might occur when customers always order 100 a month. From a load-leveling perspective, it may be more efficient to produce 25 a week.

I worked with a company that printed national magazines. They printed a million at a time (big batch). But the bindery could only glue or staple 200,000 a day (smaller batch). The other 800,000 (overproduction and unnecessary inventory) had to be stored somewhere (unnecessary movement), where they could be hit by passing forklifts (waste and rework). By switching to a *quick changeover process*, they could print 250,000 the first day and an additional 200,000 each subsequent day until they had met the volume required. This made it easier to schedule other, higher profit jobs between runs. It eliminated unnecessary inventory and motion. If they discovered a printing error in the bindery (waste and rework), they didn't have to reprint the entire magazine run.

I worked with a hospital lab. We had the lab techs wear pedometers for a week and record their travel distances. Techs were walking *two-to-four miles a day* (unnecessary motion) in the 2400 sq. ft. lab. By rearranging the machines in the lab, putting the highest volume ones into work cells, we were able to reduce movement by over 50 percent saving an estimated seven hours of delay per day, accelerating diagnosis, treatment and discharge of patients.

www.qimacros.com/Moneybelt/lean-spaghetti-diagram.html

I worked with a computer operations group that couldn't get nightly batch processing done in time to bring up the online systems in the morning. They thought they were going to have to buy a new mainframe computer at a cost of several million dollars. After laying out the nightly process, we found 32 decision points where the process waited on a technician to verify and release the next job in the string. A new employee suggested that the computer's operating system could handle most of these checks (employee wisdom). By giving 30 of the 32 decisions to the computer system, *the nightly batch run fell from nine hours to just one.*

www.qimacros.com/Moneybelt/value-stream-mapping-computer-operations.html

These opportunities exist in every business.

So, there you have it, the essence of hacking Lean—eliminate the arrows. There's a lot more depth to be explored, but for most companies, delays are the number one problem. Once those are gone, you'll be ready for ways to reduce unnecessary movement of people and materials. When that's done, you can refine the steps in the process, but first, spend some time simplifying and streamlining the existing process. And there are added benefits.

Lean's Secret Byproduct

One of the lesser known byproducts of simplifying and streamlining the process is a **50 percent reduction in defects**. When employees don't have to pick up where they left off, remember where they were, do something and set the product or service back down to wait for the next step in processing, when they can handle it using one-piece flow, they have *no* opportunity to make a mistake, miss a step or do a step twice. The chance of error falls dramatically.

People sometimes ask: "Jay, should I start with Lean or Six Sigma?" I say if delays are costing you customers, start with Lean. Defect reduction is a byproduct. It doesn't take a lot of fancy tools or methods. The process is simple.

Lean: Simplify and Streamline the Process

1. 5S the workspace.

2. Map the Value Stream paying special attention to the delays between work activities.

3. Map unnecessary movement of people and products using a Spaghetti Diagram.

4. Redesign to eliminate the delays.

5. Redesign to eliminate unnecessary movement.

6. Redesign for one-piece flow.

7. Repeat until you can *just do it now!*

Video Learning (one hour)

Watch the Lean Videos at:

http://www.qimacros.com/Moneybelt/what-is-lean-video.html

Practice (one hour): Use Post-it Notes® to lay out a value stream map (process) and/or spaghetti diagram (workspace) of one of your processes. How would you change it to eliminate DOWNTIME?

Improvement Team (two-four hours): Gather a team to reduce delays and movement in one of your key processes. Use Post-it Notes to develop the before and after value stream map and/or spaghetti diagram. Implement changes immediately or develop an action plan to implement them within the next week.

THE 4-HOUR SIX SIGMA HACK

Learning effectively requires massive elimination and removal of options. —Timothy Ferriss

Can you learn *every* method and tool of Six Sigma in four hours? Of course not. Can you, however, learn the Magnificent Seven tools that will solve 99 percent of the key business problems? You bet. And, with the right software (QI Macros), you can learn them in less than four hours and start making immediate improvements.

> *There is simply no limit on better.* -Matthew E. May

Defects

Where Lean focuses on the delays *between* process steps, Six Sigma focuses on the steps where defects and deviation occur. Defects and deviation are the enemies of productivity and profitability. A defective product is infinitely more costly than one that works right the first time. Like it or not, every process produces defects. Defects aren't spread all over a company like cream cheese on a bagel. They are more like mold growing in one corner or another. To eliminate defects requires laser focus, which brings us to the 4-50 Rule.

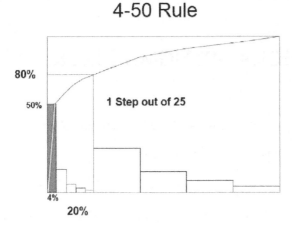

4-50 Rule

The 4-50 Rule:

Four percent of any business (one step out of every 25) causes over 50 percent of the mistakes, errors, hitches, glitches, waste and rework.

Simple tools like control charts and Pareto charts can laser focus improvement efforts on just the four percent causing the bulk of the problem. A SWAT (fast reaction) team of employees can usually figure out the root causes and countermeasures to solve the problem in a matter of hours.

www.qimacros.com/Moneybelt/six-sigma-4-50-rule-video.html

The Dark Side of the 4-50 Rule – 50 percent of an unfocused, widespread Six Sigma effort will only yield 4 percent of the benefit which leads to cancellation of Six Sigma. Don't let this happen to you; use data (i.e., facts and figures) to laser-focus the improvement effort for maximum results with minimum effort.

Six Sigma Tar Pit: Trying to create a new *measurement* system. If defects matter to the business, someone is already tracking them. Use the data that's already available to save time and start getting results immediately.

Four-Minute Six Sigma Hack

> *The most dramatic way to improve productivity is to go down to your local computer store and buy off-the-shelf, cheap, powerful shrink-wrap software. Such tools must emphasize ease of use for the casual user not a professional.*
>
> - Frederick Brooks *The Mythical Man Month*

Every million-dollar improvement project I've ever worked on began with Excel PivotTables. So, to maximize the results from Six Sigma, you will first need to summarize your data using QI Macros

79

Data Mining Wizard. www.qimacros.com/Moneybelt/six-sigma-pivottable-projects-video.html

Once you have summarized the data, finding and solving problems with defects involves four main tools used in this order: 1) control charts, 2) Pareto charts 3) Ishikawa or fishbone diagrams and 4) matrix diagrams (countermeasures and action plans). QI Macros can create these easily in Microsoft Excel. Download a 30-day trial at https://www.qimacros.com.

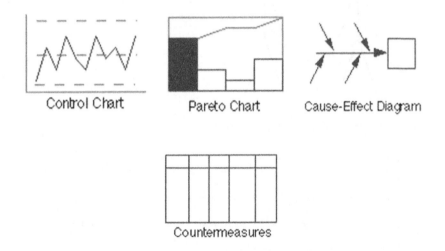

Control Chart   Pareto Chart   Cause-Effect Diagram

Countermeasures

Here's the 4-minute Six Sigma hack: the QI Macros Data Mining Wizard will take raw data about defects and create most of your improvement project for you: PivotTables, control chart, Pareto charts and fishbone diagram. Then you can decide how best to proceed. https://www.qimacros.com/training/videos/data-mining-wizard/

FIRST, CHART YOUR PERFORMANCE

Begin by tracking the number of defects (mistakes, errors, or glitches) that occur *over time*. Control charts, like a heart monitor, will track the rise and fall of defect rates, identifying when a process starts to get into trouble and enable rapid response to prevent a catastrophic failure.

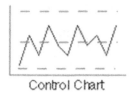

Control Chart

Six Sigma Tar Pit: Using data that has been summarized by week, month or quarter. The detail needed for analysis has been lost. Start with the raw data and use the QI Macros Data Mining Wizard.

For non-manufacturing companies, the most common control chart will be the XmR (individuals and moving range) chart. This chart can monitor cycle or turnaround times per order. It can monitor defect rates (defects per 100, 1000 or 1,000,000 units). It can monitor costs like billing adjustments. Attribute charts like the c, p and u charts can also monitor defects, but first master the XmR.

www.qimacros.com/Moneybelt/control-chart.html.

THEN, NARROW YOUR FOCUS

Once the process is stable, count and group defects into various types or categories. These show up on a Pareto chart as the "big bars." A few "big bars" out of many indicates that there are one or more problems to solve.www.qimacros.com/Moneybelt/pareto-chart.html

Six Sigma Tarpit: If all the bars are of equal height (a flat Pareto), there is nothing special going on. You haven't found the 4% causing 50% of the defects. Trying to solve problems based on a "parflato" chart is a waste of time, but teams often try:

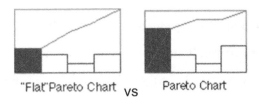

"Flat" Pareto Chart vs Pareto Chart

DATA COLLECTION

Given sufficient data about defects, this analysis can be done in a matter of minutes or hours. If not, it may take a week or two of collecting data to enable analysis, but it doesn't take months or years. You don't have to wait on measurement systems to be built and installed. Simple manual data collection using a check sheet will suffice.

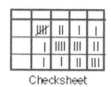

Checksheet

www.qimacros.com/lean-six-sigma-articles/data-collection

FISHBONE OR ISHIKAWA DIAGRAMS

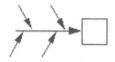

Cause-Effect Diagram

www.qimacros.com/Moneybelt/root-cause-analysis-video.html

Each "big bar" of the Pareto chart becomes the head of a fishbone, Ishikawa or cause-effect diagram. Once you know what problem you're trying to solve, it's easy to figure out who should be on the root cause analysis team. Until you've narrowed your focus using control and Pareto charts, *it's impossible to know who should be on a team!*

Six Sigma Tar Pit: Never convene a team without a laser-focused problem to solve or it will be more likely to fail and discredit Six Sigma.

Six Sigma Tar Pit: Never let a team work on more than one "big bar" at a time. Trying to analyze the root causes of multiple bars rarely works and often leads to whalebone diagramming.

SWAT teams meet for a few hours to identify the *root causes* of the problem and *countermeasures*. Disband the root cause analysis team and form an implementation team. Choose a project manager to run the implementation. Keep your Money Belt's focused on solving problems, not implementing solutions.

Six Sigma Tar Pit: If the team starts *whalebone diagramming*—filling a conference room with sheets and sheets of causes, the problem wasn't narrowly focused enough using Pareto charts. **Stop!** Back up and narrow the focus using additional, lower-level Pareto charts.

IMPLEMENTATION

Depending on the changes required, the implementation team may include some or none of the root-cause team's members. Implementing countermeasures can take minutes or months. Simple process changes can be implemented immediately. IT system changes may take months to schedule, test and implement.

VALIDATION

Once the countermeasures have been put in place, just track the defect rates and types to determine if the problem has been reduced or eliminated.

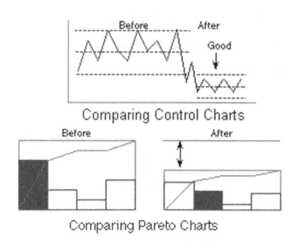

Comparing Control Charts

Comparing Pareto Charts

If performance has improved, great! If not, the team didn't find the real root causes. If the error rate has fallen to zero (perfect), stop, otherwise analyze the next "big bar."

A defect-reduction project should be able to figure out how to eliminate defects in a few hours, not months or years. Using data to laser-focus the improvement is the key to pinpointing and eliminating defects.

DEVIATION

In a manufacturing environment, Six Sigma focuses on reducing *variation*, but I think that variation sounds too benign. *Deviation* points to the product or service deviating from the perfection customers now expect. Deviation results in warranties, recalls, returns, scrap, waste and rework that devour productivity and profitability.

Finding and solving problems with deviation involves four tools used in this order: 1) control charts, 2) histograms 3) fishbone diagrams and 4) matrix diagrams (countermeasures and action plans). QI Macros can draw these charts easily in Microsoft Excel.

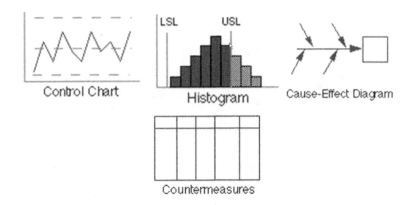

Control Chart   Histogram   Cause-Effect Diagram

Countermeasures

In service industries, most deviation involves cycle time or turnaround time. In other words, it takes too long to deliver the service. Lean can slash cycle time by eliminating unnecessary delays and movement. Control charts and histograms are excellent ways to display improved performance. Mapping the value stream or process flow will be the quickest way to solve these problems. Gather process subject matter experts in a room for a few hours to map the current process and redesign to eliminate delays, eliminate unnecessary movement, eliminate inventory and deliver one-piece flow.

In manufacturing, deviation involves adjustments in methods, materials and machines to perfect the product. If you're in manufacturing, you already probably know how to do this or you would be out of business. However, you may still have too many problems caused by order errors, billing errors, etc. Focus the tools of quality on *all* of the support functions that turn your perfect product into a nightmare for the customer.

FIRST, ANALYZE CURRENT PERFORMANCE

Manufacturing companies use XbarR charts and histograms to monitor stability and capability of production processes that suffer from deviation.

www.qimacros.com/Moneybelt/six-sigma-spc-auto-xbarr-chart-video.html

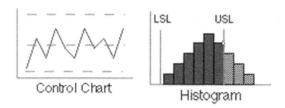

Control Chart   Histogram

Four-minute Six Sigma deviation hack: Use QI Macros Capability Suite to create a control chart and histogram of the current performance. If, and only if, the process is stable (no special causes), continue to analyze capability.

87

QI Macros histograms provide two key indicators of how well a product meets the customer's requirements: Cp and Cpk. Cp evaluates if the process will fit *within* the customer's specifications. Cpk evaluates how *centered* the process is on the target value. Cp and Cpk should be greater than 1.33 (4-sigma), preferably 1.66 (5-sigma) or 2.0 (6-sigma). QI Macros will calculate these for you. No formulas required.

www.qimacros.com/Moneybelt/six-sigma-spc-histograms-Cp-Cpk-video.html

Service companies will most often use an XmR chart to analyze turnaround times. The upper specification limit (USL) is the maximum allowed. There is no lower specification limit (LSL). Histograms will show how close each process comes to delivering the service *now*.

THEN, ANALYZE CAUSES OF DEVIATION

SWAT teams analyze root causes of deviation using Ishikawa/fishbone diagrams. This can be done in a matter of hours.

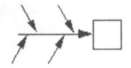

Cause-Effect Diagram

VALIDATION

Once countermeasures have been put in place, teams track deviation to determine how much the problem has been reduced or eliminated.

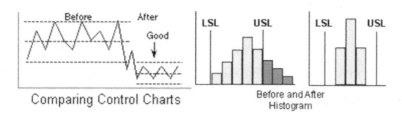

Comparing Control Charts

Before and After Histogram

If performance has improved, great! If not, the team did not find the real root causes. If the deviation has fallen to zero (perfection in Six Sigma is 3.4 defects per million), stop, otherwise continue analysis.

THE JOURNEY TO PERFECTION (SIX SIGMA)

Most companies think that because it's taken a long time to get to their current level of quality that it will take a lot longer to get to Six Sigma. Not true. By laser-focusing improvements on the 4% of the business producing over 50% of the defects and deviation (4-50 Rule), companies can go from their current 3-sigma performance to 5-sigma performance in 18-24 months.

> *Don't try to fix everything; just fix the "vital few" things of critical importance.*
>
> -Jay Arthur

Once a company has made the leap from 3-to-5 sigma, the next step will involve developing more expertise. In the rise from 3-to-5 sigma, employees with the drive and passion required to become a Six Sigma Green or Black Belt will become apparent. Send them to advanced training and focus their attention on the next round of improvement projects. Going from 5-to-6 sigma will take a greater depth of methods and tools than are presented here.

This is the Agile Six Sigma Hack—use QI Macros and a few key tools to rapidly go from 3-to-5 Sigma. Don't waste time training multicolored belts until you discover who loves improvement. (Hint: not everyone does.)

Video Learning (2-3 hours)

Watch the Six Sigma videos and case studies at:

www.qimacros.com/Moneybelt/toc.html

Do the practice exercises using the QI Macros to practice creating control charts, Paretos and histograms.

Data Analysis (one hour): Find some data about defects, mistakes and errors in your business (look at QI Macros pivottable.xlsx or datamining.xlsx files for examples). Use the QI Macros Data Mining Wizard to create a PivotTable (defects), control chart (defects or deviation) and Pareto chart (defect types) or histogram (deviation) of the process. Then figure out who should be on the root cause analysis team.

Improvement SWAT Team (two-four hours): Gather a team to reduce defects or deviation in one of your key processes. Use the data analysis—control charts, pareto charts or histograms—to laser-focus the improvement effort. Conduct a root cause analysis. Use an Ishikawa/fishbone diagram to show the results of root cause analysis. Use countermeasures and action plans to identify the improvements. Implement changes immediately or within the next week. Use the same control chart and Pareto chart or histogram to verify that the improvement worked.

AGILE PROCESS INNOVATION MANIFESTO

I worked with a metal manufacturer grossing $200 million a year. They had been using Lean, but not Six Sigma. Why just Lean and not Six Sigma?

Like many other companies, they thought Six Sigma would take too long, cost too much and not deliver results. Sadly, for most Six Sigma implementations, *this is true*. It's one of the reasons so many Six Sigma implementations fail in the first three years.

The Holy Grail for anyone who runs a company, service or manufacturing, is *fast, affordable, flawless execution*.

Flawed execution is costly in time, money and customers. *Flawless* execution is priceless to you and your customer.

We live in a world where employees actively resist change. So, it's imperative to stop trying to *change* them and, instead, create an environment where they participate in changing the process to achieve flawless execution.

LEAN SIX SIGMA CAN BE FAST, SIMPLE AND AMAZING

I worked with the metal manufacturing company's leadership team for just three days. The first day, we focused on learning the essential methods and tools of Six Sigma using QI Macros® In the afternoon, we started analyzing their data about defects like inclusions in the finished product. The next day teams dove into solving key production and delivery problems.

After just a few hours using QI Macros with my bare-bones, laser-focused *Agile* Lean Six Sigma process, the team had developed three killer improvement projects revolving around cycle time and defects. The only thing left to do was implement the changes and measure results. This company is on track to cut scrap from 12 to less than 7 percent saving millions.

If you have tools like QI Macros and some data about delay, defects and deviation, it's easy to find the *"invisible* low hanging fruit" in any business.

What's Wrong with DMAIC?

DMAIC is a simple process to understand—Define, Measure, Analyze, Improve and Control. Steps are completed one at a time which presupposes that you need to start at the beginning with Define leading to Measure and so on. Each step is clearly delineated which makes it easy to manage, but you don't get improvements until late in the process.

Consider that in most cases companies already have tons of data about delays, defects and deviation. What they lack is the ability to analyze the data. So, you don't need to Define the problem or create new Measurements (DM); you just need to be able to Analyze, Improve and Control (AIC).

The Three Silent Killers of Productivity and Profits

Ask any business owner or executive, they know that something is killing productivity and profits, but that it is hard to put a finger on the culprit. While many people look for *someone* to blame, the problem is rarely a person. Invariably it's the *system or process*.

In any business, there are three silent killers of productivity and profitability:

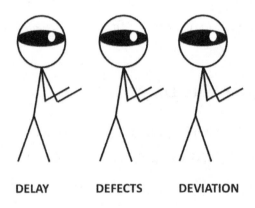

DELAY   **DEFECTS**   **DEVIATION**

Delays: Most business processes grow up in an ad-hoc fashion over time. They involve too many workarounds and rework loops. They suffer from too many *unnecessary* delays between steps.

Delays are killing your productivity and profitability.

Defects: Like it or not, every process produces defects. Even a profitable business can suffer from a three-percent error rate across sales, marketing, ordering, fulfillment, invoicing, etc. These defects are costing a typical business *one-third of total revenues.*

Defects are killing your productivity and profitability.

Deviation: Some products are a little too big or too small, too long or too short, too wide or too narrow. Some customer service processes take too long or cost too much. These are all forms of deviation (i.e., variation from a customer's ideal target value). Deviation results in warranties, recalls, returns, scrap, waste and rework that devour profits.

Deviation is killing your productivity and profitability.

Simple tools like control charts, Pareto charts and histograms can diagnose problems with defects and deviation. Employee SWAT teams can quickly identify the root causes of these kinds of problems and implement countermeasures. In Agile, this is known as a *sprint.*

Once these problems are solved, productivity and profitability begin to flow easily from the business. It plugs the leaks in your cash flow. And, best of all, it helps to distinguish your company in the marketplace. Customers appreciate fast, affordable, flawless services and products, and they will tell their friends.

Most people think that problems are spread evenly all over the business. They are wrong. You don't have to fix everything in your business. To maximize results and minimize costs, you have to focus on the few key places causing most of the delay, defects and deviation which causes the most lost profit and productivity.

LEARN TO FISH

I "grew up" in the time between the end of TQM and the beginning of Six Sigma. I developed my own acronym for improvement. My secret to Lean Six Sigma is learning how to use performance measurements to FISH—Focus, Improve, Sustain and Honor:

Focus: Laser-focus the improvement effort, because problems aren't spread all over your business, they are clustered in small areas that you can find and fix. There are hidden gold mines in your business, but you will need the tools of Agile Lean Six Sigma to find them!

Laser focus requires only a handful of methods and tools. You can learn these methods and tools in a matter of hours at:

www.agileprocessinnovation.com

Improve: Analyze the root causes and make improvements that will systematically cut costs and boost profits by $25 or more out of every $100 you spend.

- To eliminate unnecessary delays, you need Post-it Notes®.

- To reduce or eliminate defects and deviation you will need control charts, Pareto charts and histograms. These are easily created in Microsoft Excel using the QI Macros (www.qimacros.com/excel-spc-software).

Sustain: Monitor and maintain the new, higher level of improvements; otherwise you'll fall back into old habits and lower levels of performance. To sustain the improvement, your employees will need control charts, Pareto charts and histograms. Again, use the QI Macros control chart templates for monitoring performance.

Honor: Honor your progress. Recognize and reward improvements. Refocus and start on a new problem or issue.

YOUR FIX-IT FACTORY

Every company has two factories and I use the word "factory" loosely. It's not about manufacturing or services; it applies to any business process:

- One factory creates and delivers your product or service.

- The other, hidden, "Fix-it" factory cleans up all the mistakes and errors that occur in the main factory.

If you're a 3-Sigma company (and most companies are no better than 3-Sigma), the Fix-it Factory is costing you $25-$40 of every $100 you spend.

If you're a $1 million company, that's $250,000-$400,000. In a $10 million company, that's $2.5-$4 million that could be added back to your bottom line. If you're a $100 million company, that's $25-40 million Just think what saving a fraction of that money could do for your productivity and profitability! You need only a few methods and tools to do it.

My advice: Spend a few hours learning and applying the "Magnificent Seven" tools that will solve most problems, *and then* add in the tools from the long-tail, either through training, reading a book or online resource.

Using these tools you can move rapidly from 3-sigma to 5-sigma using maps of work flow, a few key problem solving tools (control chart, Pareto chart, histogram and root cause analysis), and control charts to monitor and sustain the improvements.

BE A MONEY BELT!

If you have sluggish, error-prone processes that irritate customers *and* employees, those processes are consuming a *third or more* of your revenues and preventing business growth.

No one can afford to spend months or years implementing Lean Six Sigma. Most people can't afford the time or money to attend the 10-20 day trainings. It's overkill. You can, however, learn the essential tools quickly and start using them immediately. www.agileprocessinnovation.com.

ARE YOU AN AGILE PROCESS INNOVATION SUCCESS STORY?

I've lived through wall-to-wall, floor-to-ceiling implementations of Lean Six Sigma methods. I've made all of the mistakes and learned how to avoid them. The methods and tools are easy; getting people to want to use them is hard. So, I've had to find ways to make it as fast, affordable and flawless as possible.

From my perspective, there are too many people trained and certified as belts. Too many teams started. And not enough results. This causes most Lean Six Sigma programs to die after about three years.

The hype, jargon and mass trainings normally associated with Lean Six Sigma aren't necessary to achieve dramatic, lasting improvements quickly.

WHY IS AGILE PROCESS INNOVATION SO IMPORTANT?

1. In a winner-take-all global economy, if you aren't willing to chase the dream of fast, affordable, flawless execution, someone else will. The early adopters achieve an unbeatable lead.

2. We waste too much time, money and resources fixing stuff that shouldn't be broken.

3. The profit from plugging the leaks in your cash flow is huge— a third or more of total revenues.

4. The productivity that comes from plugging the leaks in your cash flow is also huge—2X, 4X, even 8X improvements are possible.

5. Fast, affordable, flawless companies will create an unstoppable economy in those countries that jump on the Agile Process Innovation bandwagon.

FIVE WAYS AGILE PROCESS INNOVATION CAN HELP YOU:

1. When customers realize that they don't have to wait for your product or service they will tell everyone they know, and those people will beat a path to your door.

2. When customers realize that there are no hidden costs for repairs, returns or other issues with your product or service, word of mouth and *word of mouse* will fill your store.

3. When your do-it-yourself product goes together effortlessly without missing parts or pieces, customers will love you.

4. When your restaurant customers get exactly what they ordered, quickly, with an accurate bill every time, they will encourage their friends to try it.

5. When your software and operating system never crash, hang or stall, that company will win your repeat business.

Use this book with the video training at

www.agileprocessinnovation.com. Every quick video of key methods and tools will be short—under 10 minutes. You can watch them over and over again as needed to learn the methods and tools.

There will be case studies you can download to test your skills.

You might be wondering, Jay why are you giving this video training away for free?

1. First, it's just not possible to train 99% of the world's population in Money Belt Skills even if I started today and trained 100s of trainers. *But it is possible online.*

2. Second, many people who want Lean Six Sigma training can't afford it. But they can afford Money Belt training because it's free. Or they can't afford the one-to-four weeks it takes to get the traditional Lean Six Sigma training. No one can afford to spend 14 weeks solving a problem.

3. Third, Six Sigma requires software to analyze the data in ways that pinpoints where to make improvements. While I'm offering a free 30-day trial of the QI Macros software at www.qimacros.com, I hope everyone will buy a copy because they will need it to find and fix the problems that consume a third or more of total revenue. Then they will need QI Macros control charts to monitor and sustain the improvement.

    Finally, you might consider having us analyze some of your data to focus your initial improvement efforts: https://www.qimacros.com/services/shortcut-to-results/.

4. And, if nothing else, a faster, better, cheaper experience in every restaurant and business you do business with would

make your time on this planet much more pleasant. Aren't you tired of being part of someone else's Fix-It Factory?

Four-Hour Money Belts who can help companies get closer to free, perfect and now will always be in demand.

Be a Money Belt!

Implementing Agile Process Innovation

Let's face it, nobody wants Lean Six Sigma. Companies want the bottom-line, profit-enhancing results they think Lean Six Sigma will deliver.

Companies are asking: "Isn't there a better way to implement Lean Six Sigma?" The 10-to-20 day "belt"

certifications that span several months are too expensive and slow for most companies.

I say, "Companies don't need lots of training and belts; they need 'Money Belts' who can find ways to save time and money and add those savings to the bottom line." To make it easier for employees and companies to deploy Six Sigma without the high costs, I've developed a complete, no-cost, four-hour Money Belt video training at www.agileprocessinnovation.com.

As I've suggested in this manifesto, Agile Process Innovation consists of four main steps:

- **Simplify** – 5S the process

- **Streamline** – Use Value Stream Maps and Spaghetti Diagrams to eliminate delay and movement.

- **Optimize** – Use QI Macros and the Magnificent Seven Tools of Lean Six Sigma to eliminate defects and deviation.

- **Innovate** – As processes become more effective and efficient, better ways to handle the whole process will reveal themselves. Prototype the new process and implement it.

Companies are asking: "How soon can I get results?" Most Six Sigma folklore suggests it will take months or years.

I say: "One-to-five days." I have helped teams solve million-dollar problems in anywhere from a few hours to a few days using Lean Six Sigma Demystified and QI Macros. I helped one hospital system save $5 million a year in just five days using Lean Six Sigma for Hospitals and QI Macros

Companies are turning away from certifying "belts." Healthcare companies are training "improvement advisors" rather than certifying belts because adding certifications to an employee's resume leads to turnover, not improvement. Since the recession, companies would rather hire Six Sigma expertise than spend time training existing employees.

Companies are balking at buying expensive Six Sigma software. Six Sigma trainers across America have been calling about QI Macros because their clients are asking for more affordable Six Sigma software that works in Excel. QI Macros is an easy-to-use Excel add-in that will do all of the math, graphs and statistics for Six Sigma. Companies can buy 10 copies of QI Macros for the price of a one copy of big name statistical packages.

Employees balk at learning Six Sigma formulas and statistics.

I say: "You don't need to know electrical engineering to turn on a light switch. So, you don't need to be a statistician to do Six Sigma. Drawing charts and graphs should be as easy as clicking your mouse." QI Macros has four powerful "wizards" that demystify data analysis, statistics and charts.

Lean Six Sigma needs to drink its own Kool-Aid and slash cycle time, delays, defects and deviation to achieve results faster than most people believe is possible.

START USING THE MAGNIFICENT SEVEN TOOLS TO SOLVE PROBLEMS NOW!

What are you waiting for?

- You can learn the Magnificent Seven methods and tools in one day.

- It doesn't cost a fortune. It's *free* at

  www.agileprocessinnovation.com.

  The training is FREE. Certification, however, will incur a small fee.

  Start with the Yellow Belt Certification.

- Your software should do most of the thinking for you. It should help you select the right chart, analyze the data and point you in the right direction. And it shouldn't cost a fortune. Download a 30-day trial at www.qimacros.com or buy a copy at www.qimacros.com/store.

WHAT IF YOU DON'T WANT TO LEARN LEAN SIX SIGMA OR QI MACROS?

Great! We can take your data and turn it into an improvement project *ready for analysis*. No waiting! We will need *raw data* about defects, mistakes and errors. We will need the what, where, when, how, who and how much about each defect, but then we can turn it into a "ready to bake" improvement project. (We can't do the root cause analysis for you; that's your job.) Start Now:

https://www.qimacros.com/services/shortcut-to-results/

PROCESS INNOVATION

Process innovation is often harder to accomplish than one might expect. The answers rarely lie within your industry or business. Every business suffers from the "curse of knowledge:" You know too much about how your business is supposed to work. The answers you want are often found outside of your industry.

Kodak invented the digital camera but could not capitalize on it. Xerox invented the mouse and icon-based computer screens we use today but couldn't capitalize on it. Most Baby Bell telephone companies couldn't grasp the significance of cellular or cable and missed out on the opportunity of a lifetime. Too often industries become blind to changes around them. Marriott didn't invent Airbnb. Quality improvement, TQM and Lean Six Sigma suffer from the same myopia.

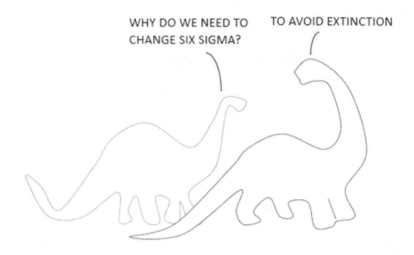

The software industry adapted insights from Lean manufacturing to create Agile software engineering. I'm suggesting that we can adapt the insights from Agile software and apply them to Lean Six Sigma to get a robust, high-performance way to simplify, streamline and optimize any business process.

I have found that through repeated cycles of simplification and optimization that revolutionary ways to deliver products or services will jump out at you. There are many tools in the Six Sigma toolkit to help with defining and implementing this new way of doing business—voice of the customer (VOC), quality function deployment (QFD) and others.

One of the easiest ways to get going is develop a transition matrix describing where you are now and the journey to world-class performance. You will want to look at other industries to find ways to transform your business.

TRANSITION PLANNING

Change management begins by asking: "Where are we?" and "Where do we want to be?" To fill in the blanks between the current state and desired state we ask a third question: "How do we get there?"

The QI Macros Transition Planning Matrix provides a tool and a method for answering all three questions. You can find the Transition Planning Matrix under Lean Six Sigma Templates, Planning Tools. While you may not need the whole transition planning matrix for every improvement, it will help you think about the change in a more robust way.

Where Are You? Where Do You Want To Be?

The Transition Planning matrix has a column to describe the current environment and one to describe the future desired environment. While it's often easy to describe the current state of affairs, it takes some thinking and Post-it notes to describe the desired state.

How Do You Get There?

Four key steps describe most transitions involving Lean Six Sigma Projects:

1. Simplify and Streamline (Lean)

2. Optimize (Six Sigma)

3. Expand into New Domains (Innovation)

4. Competitive Advantage (pulling ahead of the competition)

Most changes will require changes to people, processes and technology.

SPOT - Strategy, Process, Organization and Technology

The transition planning matrix has four main sections: Strategy, Process, Organization and Technology (SPOT) that describe the key elements of a business transition.

Strategy

Business strategy consists of three key elements: innovation, improvement and impression. To survive and thrive, businesses need to *maximize* one of these elements to establish their uniqueness and *optimize* the other two in service of the core strategy. Apple is known for *innovation*. Wal-Mart is known for *improvement and operational efficiency.* Nordstrom is known for *impression and customer satisfaction.* Steve Jobs was known for innovation, but Tim Cook made

TRANSITION PLAN For: SPOT - Strategy, Process, Organization and Technology	FROM	Process Title					TO
STRATEGY (Differentiate by maximizing one of the following)	Current Environment	Simplify, Streamline and Standardize	Optimize	Expand into New Domains	Competitive Advantage	Becoming World Class
Operational Effectiveness (speed, quality, low cost, high value) Lean Six Sigma	The Discipline of Market Leaders (Treacy & Wiersema) suggests that	Increasing complexity often requires initial simplification using the five S's of Lean Thinking	Then optimize your strategy, process, organization, and technology using Six Sigma	Successful business evolution invites application in new arenas	Which brings competitive advantage	Which leads to market leadership in your choosen field
Customer/Employee Satisfaction	a company's strategy must MAXIMIZE customer satisfaction, operational					
Innovation	efficiency, OR Innovation and OPTIMIZE the other two in support of it.					
Driving Force Product Driven Customer Specific Market Specific Production Capability Technology/Know-how Sales/Marketing Distribution Natural Resource Size/Growth Return/Profit	Examples Automobiles Travel Agents Hospital Supply Printers 3M, Microsoft Mary Kay Internet Oil, gas, mining					
(Instructions)	Describe Current State of your business for each item	Businesses become complex, so first steps are often simplifying and stabilizing	Make "Quantum Improvements" in speed, quality, and cost, to optimize performance	Leverage efficiency and effectiveness into new products, services, and markets	Use core competencies to establish competitive advantage	Become the company everyone benchmarks for excellence in your chosen niche

Apple the operational excellence juggernaut that it is today.

Is your change about innovation, improvement or impression? How will this affect your communication about it? The Strategy section will help you address this facet of change.

Process

The ability to consistently deliver a product or service is a function of process. This section of the Transition Planning Matrix covers essential business processes. There are six key processes: 1) understanding the customer's needs and wants (i.e., voice of the customer), 2) involving customers in design and delivery, 3) marketing and selling, 5) customer service and 6) managing customer information.

How does your change impact and improve one or more of these key business processes?

	Process Title					
ESSENTIAL PROCESSES	Current Environment	Simplify, Streamline and Standardize	Optimize	Expand Into New Domains	Competitive Advantage	Becoming World Class
Understand Your - Market Environment - Customer Needs and Wants - Segment Customers (Customer Satisfaction)	Six Common Processes and Best Practices Identified by Arthur Anderson (Hiebeler, et. al., 1998)					
Involve Customers in Design and Production of Products and Services - Develop New Concepts - Evaluate Prototypes - Refine and Test (Innovation)						
Marketing and Selling Products and Services - Secure Channels of Distribution - Establish Pricing - Develop Promotion Strategies - Deploy Sales Force - Process Orders - Develop Customers (Operational Effectiveness)						
Involve Customers in Product and Service Delivery - Offer Broad Delivery Options - Customize Delivery - Identify Customer Delivery Needs - Develop Distribution Capability (Customer Satisfaction, Operational Effectiveness)						
Customer Service - Point of Contact Excellence - Cross-Functional Cooperation - Improve Customer Expectations (Customer Satisfaction)						
Manage Client Information - Build Customer Profiles - Establish Service Information - Measure Customer Satisfaction (Customer Satisfaction)						

Organization

This section covers various aspects of the human element of the company and its transitional needs. Will this change the organization's structure or role? How will it affect core competencies? What changes will be required in the recognition and rewards systems? What training will be required? How will you create awareness and desire for this change?

Process Title						
ORGANIZATION (PEOPLE)	Current Environment	Simplify, Streamline and Standardize	Optimize	Expand Into New Domains	Competitive Advantage	Becoming World Class
Organizational Structure						
Organizational Role						
Accountability and Rewards						
Core Competencies						
Employee Development						

Technology

This section covers necessary technology changes like data, hardware and software. What information system changes will be required to implement your improvement? How long will that take? How will you get IT on your side to make the changes? Are there "off-the-shelf" tools like QI Macros that can meet your needs?

	Process Title					
TECHNOLOGY	Current Environment	Simplify, Streamline and Standardize	Optimize	Expand Into New Domains	Competitive Advantage	Becoming World Class
Architecture						
Data						
Business Rules						
Software/ Hardware Environment						
Network						

Transition Planning

Once you know where you are and where you want to go, the next step is to identify all of the activities required to move all four elements of the SPOT forward, in sync, to achieve the desired future. This involves thinking, because if you try to shift the Process or Technology without a plan to get the employees on board to support it, it will fail. The forces of inertia will hold the old behavior in place.

Every step forward requires the synchronized movement of all four elements. This is why new Technology (T) often sits idle waiting for the Strategy, Process and Organization (SPO) to catch up. Or a process change waits on technology. Or an organization change doesn't have the desired effect.

Once a company starts shifting all four elements toward the desired future, it's easy to sustain the movement, but getting started is often hard.

Where do you want to be?

Every change, large or small, needs to be examined to determine what else needs to be aligned to ensure its success. I've seen too many projects fail to achieve desired results because teams forgot to align strategy, process, organization and people in service of the change. I've seen too many projects fail because the change wasn't woven into the new employee orientation training and reward systems.

The transition planning matrix helps you envision the future, identify the tarpits along the way and implement countermeasures to make sure the change survives and thrives.

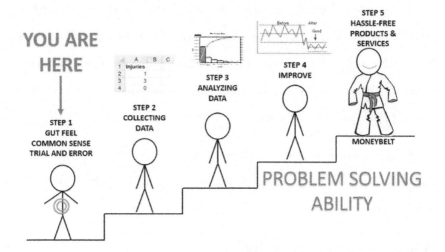

AGILE PROCESS INNOVATION MINI-MANIFESTO

Is it possible to accelerate the adoption and use of Lean Six Sigma methods and tools by *hacking Lean Six Sigma*? I believe the answer to this question is YES!

While Lean Six Sigma came from manufacturing, 80 percent of American businesses are service businesses. Can these businesses use a subset of Lean Six Sigma methods and tools to maximize results? Yes, again.

Traditional Lean Six Sigma implementations take months or even years to see results:

Traditional Lean Six Sigma

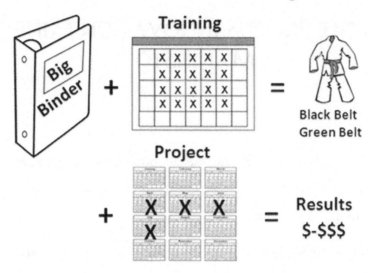

Agile Lean Six Sigma training takes a different approach. Using existing defect data and software, we can train employees in a day or less *and* solve real problems:

Agile Lean Six Sigma

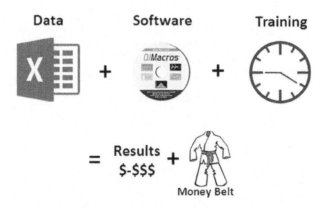

I'm an Agile Lean Six Sigma Process Innovator!
I value:

- **Results** over rigor

- **Working improvements** over comprehensive documentation

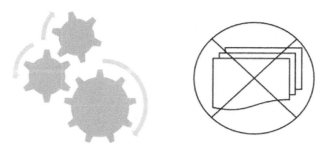

Cross-functional collaboration over silo analysis

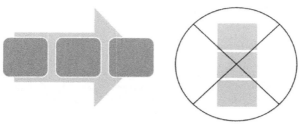

- **Responding to change** over following a plan

- **Numerous small experiments** over a few large bets

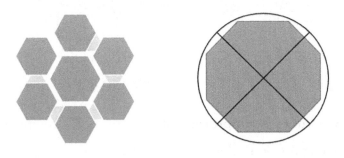

- **Testing, data and charts** over opinions and conventions

- **Engagement and transparency** over posturing

Agile Lean Six Sigma Principles

1. **Satisfy customers** by early and continuous delivery of valuable improvements

2. **Welcome changing requirements**, even late in the improvement

3. **Deliver working improvements frequently** (in hours or days rather than weeks)

4. **Close, daily cooperation** between business people and improvers

5. **Build projects around motivated individuals**, who should be trusted

6. **Face-to-face conversation** is the best form of communication (co-location)

7. **Working improvement is the primary measure of progress**

8. **Sustainable improvements**, able to maintain a constant pace

9. **Continuous attention to technical excellence and good design**

10. **Simplicity**—the art of maximizing the amount of work *not done*—is essential

11. **Self-organizing teams** deliver the best architectures, requirements, and designs

12. **Regular reflection** helps the team become more effective and adjust accordingly

Innovative process transformations emerge from simplifying, streamlining and optimizing key processes using the Magnificent Seven Tools of Lean Six Sigma. Any attempt to "reengineer" a complex business process will fail without this prework.

AGILE PROCESS INNOVATION CHEAT SHEET

FOUR-HOUR LEAN HACK – SIMPLIFY AND STREAMLINE

5S – Sort, Straighten, Shine, Standardize, Sustain	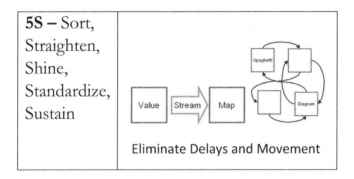

FOUR-HOUR SIX SIGMA HACK – OPTIMIZE

Focus	Four-Minute Six Sigma Hack (**Data Mining Wizard**) 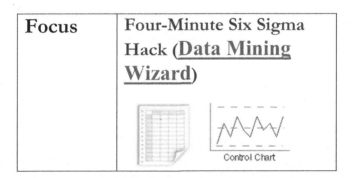

125

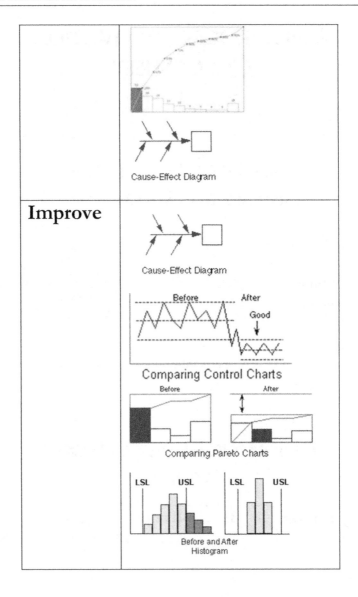

Cause-Effect Diagram

Improve

Cause-Effect Diagram

Comparing Control Charts

Comparing Pareto Charts

Before and After
Histogram

Sustain	 Comparing Control Charts
Honor	Recognize, Reward, Refocus, Repeat
Innovate	 **Innovation**

Made in the USA
Monee, IL
21 January 2024

51385176R00076